EVERYTHING SEEMS
SIGNIFICANT
THE *BLADE RUNNER* POEMS

EVERYTHING SEEMS SIGNIFICANT
THE *BLADE RUNNER* POEMS

JAN BOTTIGLIERI

BLAZEVOX[BOOKS]
Buffalo, New York

BlazeVOX [books]
131 Euclid Ave
Kenmore, NY 14217
Editor@blazevox.org

publisher of weird little books

BlazeVOX [books]

blazevox.org

21 20 19 18 17 16 15 14 13 12 01 02 03 04 05 06 07 08 09 10

BlazeVOX

Acknowledgements and thanks:

The author would like to sincerely thank the editors of the following journals, in which poems from this collection previously appeared or are forthcoming:

Ekphrastic Review:	Chapter 6: The Replicants in Question.
Atticus Review:	Chapter 7: Rachael; Voight-Kampff Test.
Mayday Magazine:	Chapter 13: Deckard's Dream.
	Chapter 18: Retirement... Witnessed.
	Chapter 20: Wake Up, Time to Die.
Court Green:	Chapter 1: Credits and Forward.
	Chapter 3: Emotional Response.
	Chapter 8: Leon's Hotel Room.
	Chapter 25: Right Moves.
	Chapter 27: No Way To Treat a Friend.
Clementine Unbound:	[You're Talking About Memories.]

For their early encouragement, I'd like to thank: Adam Riske and Mike Pomero, who clapped at my comment after that screening; Patrick Bromley, who listened, believed, and made room for me at the FTM table (I'm looking forward to your Tobe Hooper book); and the FThisMovie! community, who gave me a virtual home. For support and guidance that was more human than human, deep gratitude to Tony Trigilio. For giving me eyes that see poetry everywhere, big ups to my *RHINO* crash. Loving thanks to my father, mother, and brother for gifting me with a past; to John, for sharing with me the present; and to Jake, for writer talks and nonsequitexts, for driving me around LA to *BR* locations, and for being my artifact, my blueprint, and the bearer of imbedded memory.

TABLE OF CONTENTS/CHAPTER LIST

Everything Seems Significant
The *Blade Runner* Poems

The future enters us... in order to be transformed in us, long before it happens.

—Rilke

Credits and Forward

Fast forward, reverse, the green
Ladd Company tree
makes and unmakes itself.

Dark book of the beginning: I am trying
to change my life.

Though I've watched the film countless times
since the first in 1982, this
will be different:

I try now to see everything, write it down,
my project, I call it. Run film forward, reverse:
I want to commit

(to) memory.

* * *

From Scott: *I knew my opening shots
would be so spectacular that I didn't want
the titles to upstage them in any form.*

The green tree, line by line: dot matrix tech
from 1981 echoes back in
2018's CAD/CAM replicators:

a 3D-printer can even create
a model of an unborn child
                              (of course,
they first began doing this in Japan.)

Then full black screen, white
type(face): duality?
Everything seems significant.

The double letters of Harrison,
Emmet, Hannah, William,
Brion's odd O.

                    That O
the mouth of a caroling angel:
Those robed, frozen figures

with uptilted faces,
eyes lashed closed.
Everything seems significant.

More double letters—is it odd
most names here seem to have them? —
Joanna, Terry, Powell, Paull.

(I've wondered if Lawrence G. Paull was—is?—
related [that twin L!] to Morgan Paull,
our Holden, Deckard's doppleganger.)

DP Jordan Cronenweth, a visionary,
already diagnosed with Parkinson's,
that cureless, slow dismantling.

The soundtrack's fall as the crawl rises up
to meet it: *I had never allowed for how
magical the music would be*

says Scott on commentary. The red word
REPLICANT echoes the credits'
only other red: the film's title,

BLADE RUNNER. I pause, reverse
to the beginning, watch again
to check my memory:

reverse, reverse,
fast forward, stop. On commentary track,
art director David Snyder says

I wound up doing Blade Runner *by default
and it turned out to probably be the only thing
that will be in my obituary.*

Eye on the City

—LOS ANGELES/NOVEMBER, 2019

Fire—

mechanical landscape needled
by sparks of light.

A marginal future:
smokestacks bellow, bright exhalation.

Chimes clang, a low bass thrum;
buzzing hum of spinners,

a single bolt
from the orange sky.

Then the eye
fills the frame: blue, fixed,

flame-licked, gaze holding
a moment and back to the slow zoom:

from smog haze twin ziggurats
loom 700 stories tall, beacons blazing

up into darkness. The great eye
fills again with fire,

sweet clarion rising
into Doppler drop, apocalyptic.

Interior: Smoke and blue shadow, Holden
with his back to the camera,

eye on the city. Forced perspective,
process shot, seamless: we enter

—airborne, omnipotent—as if pulled
by the spin of the fans' black blades.

Emotional Response

> *Not you, his mother: alas, you were not the one*
> *Who bent the arch of his eyebrows into such*
> *expectation.*
>
> —Rilke

Crane shot: Holden smoking
In a shaft of blue light.

Sips his coffee, gestures
to the chair; sits, sighs, rouses
the VK. Leon—*engineer,*
waste disposal—

in backlit profile, haloed.
Then the eye fills the frame:
browngold, mutable
as memory, an aperture.

Black bellows breathe in
Leon's damp exhalation.

Child-curious: *What one? How come I'd be there?*
Holden, half-hearted, annoyed:
Maybe you're fed up. Who knows?
On its back, the tortoise struggles, exposed,

the bloodrush echoes, the trapped eye snaps
open and shut, winking like an accomplice.

On commentary, Fancher and Peoples
argue who authored the scene:
one of the best lines in moviedom,
Fancher says, *a Freudian line:*

'I'll tell you about my mother!' – *Bango!*
Peoples: *You wrote that.*

Leon, bent forward, squeezes
the trigger: then liquid gush
as Holden explodes head first
through the blown wall. *No!*

Fancher says. *Oh, I hope I didn't:*
For a long time now, I've enjoyed
disliking myself for not writing it.

Interrupted Sushi

There has to be a poem about
the White Dragon

texts Jake. I've sent him
a photo of my ramen, captioned
'*And noodles*'.

On screen, an origin. The woman
smiles, swallows her pill.

Themes emerge: *two, two, four*
Deck says, doubling down
then giving up. Gaff's cityspeak
repeated. *Tell him I'm eating.*
No choice for Deckard

but to take the bowl with him.

Something always fascinated me
Jake types: *that noodle stand looks*
miserable food is hardly gourmet
why does Deckard go back
?
He guesses *comfort food*
but how can he recall

his highchair, my face
—younger, yes—hovering above,
blue smile, the blue bowl.

Are you my angel, my little bird? I show him
how to tilt his head back and open,
feed him a noodle, another.
Not yet a year old but a good mimic:

tilts his head back, mouth open
(soft carol) catching
my eye with his, we share
the whole bowl like this.

                            Now the spinner
rises through mist. Rain veil, lens flare.
The woman smiles again.
Over the landing threshold.

Old Blade Runner Magic

Fan by the file cabinet, little windmill.
Gaff silent in gold brocade.
Deck rattles the blinds on the door.
If execution is magic, what's the spell?

Clutter, cloister: Collector Bryant
on the vellum shade with a trophy kill.
Tips two shots from the bottle he keeps.
A bad one – worst yet, says the yellow smile.

Why the microphones, clustered
like correspondents at the scene?
Why is everything shot
close-up? When he spits *skin jobs*

we know what it means. *If you're not cop
you're little people* says the man
with a rhino-foot lamp. Gaff folds
the white chicken from ash-plucked trash.

Bryant says *need* but that's not the trick.
So what makes Deckard come back?
From the Sanskrit *bhrata*, the Romany *pral*:
it means brother. *No choice?*

No choice, Pal.

Replicants in Question

Every angel is terrifying.
—Rilke

What's this? Deckard asks: not *who.*

Clever bit of exposition, to reveal the quarry
to us and Deck together, let him query Bryant
for us, our proxy, blue membrane
of smoke haze rising between them.

Nexxus 6. Each description straight
from dimestore pulp, a reduction
to function, the body's brute
uses. The heads, factory fresh,
spin as in a shop window. Skull-capped,
mute and gazeless, a sameness.

No snake tattoo, no shock of white hair,
no *hate love fear anger envy* yet.
Transformation, the interpreted world: time
cut off as failsafe. *And if
the machine doesn't work?*

Flight, light: Deckard narrows his eyes.
Spinners flare out their flame-red haloes.
The score recalls its daring first notes
—a kestrel keening—
then falls.

Rachael; Voight-Kampff Test

I think he got what he wanted out
of her, which was more than just
a look.

—Katherine Haber

You see an owl. Darkling, its wing rush
brushes the chamber's curved cheek, sketching
a path you step into. Your pocketed hand.

You meet a man at work. He unpacks
his device, canted, black as your jacket,
a dark nostalgia. On the table
a bonsai strains in its vessel. May you
ask him a personal question?

What is a personal question?

You light a cigarette. Smoke rises, catching
what sun slips through the shaded glass.
Behind the veil: your eyes lambent
as two coins. It won't affect the test.

It's your birthday. Your eyes like coins.
How can it not know what it is?

O providence, its owlish face.
Easy to speak of commerce atop
his own golden ziggurat, its twin
dimmed and looming. Factory, forge.

An experiment, nothing more says Tyrell,
naming the past *a gift* as if he'd never heard
of a mother devoured by her young.

That archeological landscape,
silent as a sphinx.

We began to recognize in them
a strange obsession —

He never names it.

Leon's Hotel Room

Champaign-Urbana, 1985:
I've taken a dingy efficiency,
my final semester, one room with bath
eight blocks off campus. Faucet's steady drip.
I grew to love it—my little meals of
ramen and Coke; my records, photos, books;
origami I'd folded, strung above
the bed—and near the door, Rick Deckard's face:

glossy, larger than life, there was no place
he could not see me. I loved the scrape
on his cheek, which I felt was real—that is,
Ford's first, then Deck's by proxy. A heal-need:
I was just off chemo, pale, prone to bruise.

Across from the Yukon, Gaff and Deck pause

in the future's perpetual rain.
Steam from grates.
1-1-8-7 Hunterwasser.

The busted fixture's cicada buzz,
the scale like a dirty teardrop. The fingertip
lifting it to light. Deck's hands dissolve

to Gaff's—crafting the crude man,
head ready to strike into flame.
Gaff must know Leon will see it.

And there Leon is, crossing
to a White Dragon, we hear
that same electric buzz

as he watches his own window.
Behind it, Deckard finds the hidden
photos, shuffles them like a tarot:

The Wheel, The Twins, The Pensive Man.
Memory—that broken god, that lens.

But if the archangel now, perilous, from behind the stars
took even one step down toward us: our own heart, beating
higher and higher, would beat us to death. Who are you?
                                                        —Rilke

Chew's Visitors

Pulsepound sound, arterial:
fingers fist
into a bluish heart   *time*

                              enough

Obelisks, fire, bicycle headlights.
the street meters' redlight orbs.
Bloodbright neon unblinks
above the Eye Works door.

Aperture, entry: Chew trailing tubes
like an eye plucked, jocular:

          Ha, yes! So little time...
          Ha, ha! So beautiful, beautiful indeed...

The eye, which inverts
the inverse, therefore righting;
which dilates, detects, discerns.
Posthole, postulator, tomb.

Roy, oracular: *Fiery the angels fell...*

but Chew only protests. Until he sees
Leon plunge his hand
into cobalt glow, vitreous, clingsome.
Leon sniffing as an animal might,
testing each newness—keen, ken.

Seeing, Chew knows them.

If Only You Could See

Score push, orchestral:
their breath chills
into vapor   *yes*

                                    questions

Sidelight, backlight, edgelight,
blue-bright and frozen.
Brain tissue: the eye works
by impulse, nerve.

Queried Chew, the pupil. The coat
Leon tears is functional, retina-thin:

          I just do eyes, see...
          ge-ge-genetic design – just eyes...

Memory, which invents
and interprets, therefore writing;
which directs, dissects, inters.
Gimlet, gantry, grave.

Roy, the ocular: *what I've seen with your eyes...*

Poor Chew, unlimitless. Stammers, freezes.
Leon plays, plops an orb on
each shoulder: angel, demon, that dumb device.
Roy grins, gleams; icy and godlike, he stretches
each moment, slowing time's fanspin reel.

Dying, Chew reveals.

Someone Else's Memories

Interstitial tunnel, blue pulse

of light. Again: *My mother? I'll tell you about...*
Deck yawning in the elevator cab's dim womb,
its warm, scarred walls. Strange shock
to learn we're not alone:

it shakes him, he fumbles his ID.
What do I need help for?

What we don't see, then see:
Face and artifice, the architecture of memory.
an abandoned building we sneak into.
in law this is called *an attractive hazard.*

As a girl I'd build houses for my dolls
from blocks, room after room—until
the day I could see only plastic, wood:
lightless, false. What had changed?

Do you want a drink? —
He makes himself a drink.

Me with my mother... Rachael offers, but already
there is no place in her he has not seen.
(The score's clear, high F: *Memories of Green*,
which I have begun to learn

on the piano I played in my mother's house.)
Finally she speaks, steps into her own
story, take it back from him,
the bad joke of him. Of home.

Do you want a drink? —
He makes her a drink.

She chickens and runs. Deckard advances
into darkness, then bends, lifts the photo.
The scene re-animates—
music, dappled shadow, light.

Blink and you'll miss it.

Pris Meets Sebastian

Angel and puppet: A real play, finally.
— Rilke

Smokeshroud, rainveil, loose layer
of gathered trash: the permeable barriers

we navigate. She slips, bumps shoulder through
glass, but is called back:

petcollar pretty, shy smile.
I'm hungry, J.F. –

She knows how to pull his
strings, what she was made to do.
Smile's fast fade when he turns,
the score's distant, injured yowl.

Pale face that beams down at them, nods.
In the cage they ascend:
alone but not lonely
though shafts of blue light.

J.F. fumbles at the door, lets Pris
enter first: boyish valor,
funny valentine.

She lies *no* about design.
Home again, home again.

His clever friends:
Kaiser wheels on his tiny black heel,
bumps his shoulder in retreat:
her sense memory, gimlet grin.

I'm sort of an orphan.
Father less, mother less, what bloodguest
has J.F. invited in? His voice
across the dark gulf of home:

can I take those things for you?

Deckard's Dream

*I wanted a sound for light. So Jimmy Shields finds a
sound for light... He'd make things out of empty milk
bottles and silver foil from a cigarette packet....
It was the artistry of the ear.*

—Ridley Scott

Dark rhino lit against white
wash of light, sweeping
sound swings through
glass white mask eyes
black metronome beats no
time sings in struck high
notes on the white
key to Deckard's past:
wife photo gun empty glass

I wanted a sound for light.

Deck drowses, then opens his eyes.
The famous white unicorn
dream (vision) (memory)
—the light-sound transforms into
bloodrush of breath.

Is that what he remembers? Is this the *why?*

The chapter only 54 seconds, I click back
to the beginning. Dark rhino as faux unicorn;
pale mask, a false face. Cluttered space:
gathered artifacts, the past in pastiche.

My first published piece:
an archeology student
treks with his professor, tracking a unicorn

he does not believe in.
The older man's life work.

When they come to a cave, only the boy
can squeeze through: his torchlight sweeps,
then settles on rot, white bone and horn.
He tells the man *There's nothing here.*

It was 1982: that June
Blade Runner came out,
nine months before my first diagnosis
(Frank Scott already two years gone:

the loss that may have pushed Ridley to drop *Dune*
and dive into the project then called *Dangerous Days*.)

On screen, Deckard's face again—

The note he strikes deepens to choirlike hum.
The animal comes: pulsepound, hoof drum
of memory, music and breath in white:

I wanted a sound for light.

Esper Enhancement

Only at times, the curtain of the pupils
lifts, quietly—. An image enters in
                                        —Rilke

Reverie—. Then image pins his glance:
he lips the photo, grabs glass and bottle.
In the clutter, blankfaced, the Esper.
Deckard clicks it to life:

He sits, fills glass from bottle,
then tilts his head. *Enhance.*
Deckard slips into a life:
A man rests, cheek on his fist.

Deck tilts forward. *Enhance—*
(stuttered shuttersound) *stop.*
He rests his cheek on his fist.
Move in – stop. Pull out, track right.

Shutter's stuttered sound. *Stop.*
Deck slips closer in—a voyeur, spy.
Center in, pull back… Track 45 right.
Unseen, the Esper's all-seeing eye:

Deckard closes in—voyeur, spy—
on the cluttered table, the glass.
Scans scene with Esper's all-seeing eye:
Same black-banded bottle

as on his own cluttered table—glass
shape like a knobbed bone, unbodied.
(So many black-band dead bottles!)
He finds the mirror to slip through:

its shape like an orbital bone, unbodied.
What is the body but confine, cage?
He uses the Esper to slip through
its bars, enter deeply the hidden.

What is the body? Confine, cage.
The woman reclines, shoulders
bare. Deck enters deeply, unbidden,
the distant room: *Stop. Enhance.*

The woman reclines, shoulders
revealed—. The image pins his glance
to the distant room. *Enhance. Hard copy right there.*
He's caught her. Takes her face from the Esper.

Manufactured Skin

The score bleeds through,
leads us to the street:
Animoid Row's steam and neon,
a swordfish, semi-flayed.

What is the body but confine, cage?
Hemmed in by skin: aperture, ailment.

The scale, still in its polythene sleeve.
Deckard offers it to the SEM:
Like the Esper, it closes in,
reveals the alien landscape—

Finest quality, superior workmanship.

When I was 10 I got what I wanted
from the Wish Book: A blue microscope
with samples and slides.

I could peek inside: through the ocular lens
down the well of the tube, the bright
mirror below forwarding light.
Flywing, feather, white corner torn
from the instruction page,

Explore New Worlds
Within Our World.

I'd learned the old world
two summers before: my father,
the broken vessel—microscopic, interior—
that felled him.

I missed him. My favorite sample
to fix beneath the coverslip:
myself. Skin, scab, lash—
what was I anymore?

On screen, the capillary alley.
Deckard steps back, unnerved,
as two ostriches are hustled past.
He taps on the glass,

is waved in by Abdul, the loupes and thick
lenses. Deck gets him to talk
by yanking his tie, that quick constriction
of breath. A *Final Cut* trick:

the words we see formed are Ben Ford's,
the son's lips laid over the father's
to fix the match—
a special effect, digital.

My *Souvenir Magazine* claims
the ostriches are mechanical.

Miss Salomé

DS: Now he looks back at what's supposed
to be the dance... I always thought Joanna
was disappointed about that. That she
really wanted to do that.
LP: That would have been hot.
　　　　—David Snyder and Lawrence Paull

the masks the veils
the smoke the veils
the man is dry

her photo with his own
her face on the vidphone
that's not my kind of place

but he lingers　then *watch her*
take the pleasures from the serpent
and he turns　visors his eyes
with his fingers

* * *

fake voice　talks himself in
the holes the snake the skin
of course it's not real

she doesn't mind being looked at
you'd be surprised / no I wouldn't
but not revealed:

handblade to his neck
yanking his tie　that quick
constriction of breath
that little death　that veil

* * *

Salomé, what is original
about sin? The animals are at home
within themselves, their skin.

Pluck a scale, affix it to your skin.

The unveiling begins: peel back, conceal,
that uneasy truce. Like memory:
that truth, mistruth.
The gaze that pushes through

still stops at the skin.

This dance
earns you a kingdom—well, half.
What is your choice? What comes into
your mind—your mother? She said
ask for it, Salomé.

They made you
dangerous, then looked away.

Pursuing Zhora

After their meet-cute—
the funny prattle, the brute straddle—
it's sweet pursuit: romantic,

isn't it, the timeworn battle
of the sexes, that dance; the coy slip,
the glance across a crowded street?

The heart pumps so it's more
than meat. Her quaint cries
as she runs.

The eye of the gun.

Retirement... Witnessed

At the second
shot time
slows:

the siren, the red
light   (in my memory

              flashing against the bright
              pane: my mother

              has sent me down to let the men
              in   and in

              the men come to carry out
              my father: my body

              struck against the wall to make
              room for his still

              living body   the stretcher
              [to carry out: as duty   burden])

at the third shot
the hole in her body blown

open: through glass
and slow what is memory

but this: now, stretched
open   her jacket flaring back

              (black night   the neighbors out
              on lawns, drawn by light)

then snow—fake
bodies dressed like hers   she falls

final, angled, clipped
-winged

                    (*like your own angel*
                    they'd tell me:

                    that missing   that all-
                    seeing)

like Leon, I was struck
open   watching it happen:

[*to bear:* as witness, as carry
to commit: as
to memory]

How Many to Go?

Bryant says to Gaff *he's a goddaaaam one
-man slaughterhouse* and then to Deck *four more
to go*. To kill. Rain like a wet kiss, dear
slickness. Deckard sways, a sickness. That's one
more than he expects; he wants nothing more
than home. *Drink some for me.* The low drone, sigh
of doors knifing down and they're gone. Only

Deck's not alone; she's changed her mind. This: dear
false past, dear downcast. Smoke lit. This: it is
everything, that blueness of goodbye.
Volta, current, riverine newness for
Rachael: to choose. A threshold, unworn. Our
making, unmaking, mind—forge and force. *Hate love
fear anger envy.* Choice is why she is

not where they look for her. Such *I don't*, such
think so. Street-song ache and cry. The way pain
begins: nervelight, a nostalgia. Bright, and

such pleasure that I'll treasure 'til I die

Wake Up. Time to Die.

Who has not sat, afraid, before his heart's
curtain? It rose: The scenery of farewell.
                                        —Rilke

To re member – re call:
bring the body back to itself, stitch
by stitch. That itch.

She's waking up
was not the first thing I'd heard:
it came after the low moan

of the body I did not recognize
as mine. At *her eyes are opening*
the surgeon paused

behind his curtain
(a bright instrument,
the body opened) until

some machine was adjusted,
hissed its accord,
and I slept. In recovery,

I told the nurse
I thought I was dying! But no —
just coming to — she refused

to admit it had happened. But I knew
what my body was bent on:
opening into the bright rain

haze from the OR lamp array, re-
membered in light, re-called
to it. Like Leon: muscleblaze

and fight, *how long will I live?*
…longer than you, slinging
Deck's body like ammunition

down the black barrel
of his past life: *painful/*
oh I agree until

Bango! his third eye
bursts open, bright neo-
cortex root-bloom rising,

a streaming forth
unfutured, unmemoried. To be
complete, complicit:

to fade and flower at once,
to know *yes* as it is happening
that *yes: it is happening*

I Owe You One

Clear spirit in the shot
glass, then the blood flash:

some wound inside
opens. *Shakes? Me too—*

so many ways to say it. (He chooses
the ~~painless~~ plainest

and strips off his shirt.)
She shivers in her damp fur.

Body as ~~altered~~ altar, aperture.
Dream as ~~memory~~ malady, viral:

maybe it's contagious, this desire
to define ourselves

as like each other. She
hasn't fevered yet.

Then he names his life
Debt: *I owe you one.*

He names it ~~Futile~~ Future.
A type of suture.

Say 'Kiss Me'

1.

When a woman enters a room, a smaller woman
enters the room beside her.

She may look into a photograph
as into a mirror, trying to place the other woman's face.

She is an instrument. Levers and hammers, machine.
She remembers lessons.

Her music is a kind of nostalgia.
When a woman enters

a dream it is in this way: by making
an old music. She doesn't know how the pattern,

that muscle memory, was set inside of her,
but it is inside of her.

2.

Memory is an inheritance:
we become our own mothers, fathers, choosing
a past. Art and fact collude.

How rain beads on a spiderweb
outside the glass of our girlhood room.

We artifact, blueprint:
what we've done is what we do.

But what if memory's
not true?

3.

(John says) *Well maybe this one should be a prose poem,
or an essay* (and I say) yes, I've been thinking that
because you know, Babe, the real rape, we never see
it *yes you've talked about this before* but every time I
think of it I get so fucking mad *that's clear* because
the REAL rape, where two men open her *can you
call it that?* file and read her past, her memories, just
enter *yeah but can you call it* her head, and I can just
imagine how nonchalant *well we never see that* it's
disgusting *sure* and YES, I do call it *but we never
see* well we know it happens and she doesn't consent
to THAT *no, she* and the fucking VK *the Voight*
—does she consent to THAT?—*Kampff, no, she*
Tyrell's like TRY HER *yeah, try her* right, he
doesn't ask, doesn't even think of her as human *well
she's not* she didn't choose her past *uh-huh* all the
lies *uh-huh* and no one ever cares about her
consent *well you seem* until we get to "say 'kiss me'"
you've mentioned this and then she GIVES IT *well
sort of* but we complain it's not enough—as if *look,
I have stuff* her kiss *to do* or her body *okay?* is all
that's important about her *so I'm just* as if the
viewer, this omnipotent eye *sure, the eye*—it's us,
you know, it's us!—*okay, just calm* has the right to
say when her consent is important, when it's
enough (now he's trying to leave) *can we please
stop talking about Blade Runner* (but I follow him
down the hall).

4.

November lightslant.
You lyrical, you loosen.
You chickened and ran.

A panther paces
behind bars. No other worlds.
Say kiss me. / Kiss me.

Are the shadows striped
by light? Or light by shadow?
I can't rely on—?

5.

The girl in the photo is dressed as a nurse:
it's me with my mother,

1969. I was trying to be beautiful
as the woman who'd bring insulin

to my brother when my parents
were gone. By six I'd learned

what a person could be: the one who needs
the needle, or the one who slips it in.

When my want was shadow-thin—
what a gift I was then! Helper, angel, *oh*

Janny, she's the easy one. I'd smile
and nod, take that pat, that pill.

Nineteen when I watched Deckard
slam that door shut with his fist

and say *say kiss me* then *kiss me/again*
and I wished I could be so

beautiful: pushed too hard against
myself, eyes blackened

with my own tears. To hear
say kiss me then to say *kiss me* then

to be kissed; to say a thing, then have it
happen. Yes: I knew I shouldn't thrill

at that rough *say kiss me* shove
that blunt force *again* love—

but (I remember) by then twice
I'd felt like I was dying

and never knew
how to say *please:*

I think I'm dying.

6.

put a whistle on
your keychain keep your
hands out of his pockets put
on a little lipstick my mother told
me *but you're young you don't need much*

7.

The past: gambit, gantry, cage. What makes you stay put.
A body, a door. What is opened or shut. Your
hands hover, two birds. Your hands
on the keys. What is *rely on?*
Again. *Kiss me.*

Only Two of Us Now

> *But tell me, who* are *they, these wanderers...?*
> —Rilke

Pris blackens her eyes.
To fashion, to fix.

Coo-coo, coo-coo! Then the flat face
ticks and behind it, the mechanical

bird folds into itself: cuckoo incognito,
masked like a thief. Surrogate,

sister, spy in the nest. Child-curious,
she cartwheels and sniffs,

preens. Peeks at a screen
that throws light.

Listen: the tune trills down
like a star-wish.

Her eyeshine and hair shock,
her acrobat smile.

Then Roy arrives, presses mouth
to mouth, that hungry smear.

Only two of us now. Chokes
like a scrap stuck. Still.

Grief the bad guest,
how it asks and asks.

..and we'll die/No we won't.
An instinct, to harbor, host:

J.F. sets the eggs to boil.

We Need You, Sebastian

J.F. sets the eggs to boil.
The music, a kind of nostalgia.
The ostrich is mechanical.

Something whispers. Roy coils
his arms around his own body.
Need is the seed in soil:

a hunger, painful,
don't you agree?
Both animal, mechanical.

Chime scale, veil, the head of a doll.
What strains in its vessel. Need
crackles, shines like shook foil,

a kestrel keening. Then the fall
to Earth, spiraled violence, a mercy.
Like mercy, need's tyrannical,

an appetite getting won't spoil.
From the limbcage Pris makes, J.F. laughs, weeps.
The chess birds aloof, almost royal.
Pre-sacrifice. *Is he good?* Roy asks. He means Tyrell.

Right Moves

*"I always love working with
anamorphic, because you have this
beautiful fall-off... the pieces are sharp,
Tyrell is just sharp, and everything's
falling away behind him."*

— Ridley Scott

I try to recall my past ascensions. Nothing comes
to mind. Even birth: my first mother pushed so hard
I fell 10 days into the future and met my new mother there.

O holy elevator:
If I rode you I would shout

I'm coming for you, God! with my mouth clamped.
Now hearing the words of the game, I fall back
to the chess boys I knew, their sweaty hands slamming
the tops of the clocks. They could speak their games too,

move from memory: like Matt who'd play four boards at once
with his back turned. *Fall back* is a thing they may have said,
or *attack*, while I watched them play after school.

Roy plays the Immortal Game;
Matt must know it. His father

owned our first VCR. We'd drive to the liquor store
on Elmhurst to rent tapes. That's what it was like then—
hard to find what we wanted to see. I can't rely on
my memory but hearing Roy speak his moves I fall back:

we're all having Cokes at Matt's and *Blade Runner* finally
is in, J.F. and Roy ascend and I'm past-pulled rushing
down, farther and fast, past twisted fibers to warp, weft—

fine, immortal smallness
(dear hereness)—

I'm re-minded, the words a kind of becoming,
that sacrifice strategy: everything rising toward
and falling back, white/black, what difference:
our fathers, mothers, gone, we know what comes next.

Prodigal Son Brings Death

A man asked for his inheritance
to make his way in the world.
As if to say *I want your life, father.*
As if to say *memory/*
that broken vessel

and he went. Lived richly and far,
until gone the inheritance
and friendless, he was
accompanying his eyes
through the slump of his life

among the despairing
and despised. And thought
better to be a slave
to my father than this.
Slunk home, sunken.

From a long way father spied son,
flew out, arms flung wide-winged.
Son said *shackle me* said
I've done questionable things.
But the father said *oh light*

of my body's heart, said *so happy*
I will kill something fat for you.
Called him *Lazarus/ex-angel.*
Called him *flame, flower, flesh-and-bone.*
Said *home.* Said *home.*

***

Owl and eyeshine. Tyrell in white,
commerce-clean. Roy steps
into light: *I want more life, father.*
As if to say *inheritance/*
that broken vessel.

Skinbound Roy, kin-starved.
A slave state: vassal.
Tyrell says *you were made*
as well as we could make you
as if to say *shackled*

to my will—academic.
He falters/a falseness.
(Even the firelight: only shook foil
and fanspin.) God the refusing,
the re-version, guttering.

Roy, birth-wet: *I've done*
questionable things. Laying-on
of his hand (yes, an un-blessing)
Tyrell says *revel* as if to say *lever*
and hammer, instrument,

 something struck, like a bargain.
Roy says *heaven*: it's both *here*
And *never*. His deep kiss: an anti-
resuscitation. Soft O like a carol.
Roy's hands make a cradle.

Roy's hands clasp, like praying.
What does the false god create
by dying? An eyelessness, open.
Roy falls again, clutching a patchwork
jacket. Every angel is terrifying.

No Way to Treat a Friend

In boyhood my brother:
blond, bodied for any game,
memories of green field run and pitch,
frozen rink flying after black puck my brother
could make friends, had that
high-school fame. I tried to learn

to give him his shot, never got the knack
(he didn't like to be touched.)
I'd knot his ties for him on my own neck
(once he barked *thanks*) before work.

But what is the body? Confine, cage.
His trap of rapid decrepitude.
His dangerous days and shit-list luck.

And when his mother (our
[only the good things]
mother) left this world, my brother:

skinsick, body-betrayed, said *fuck that*
and went right after.

                    So when Deck

—under copsmack and smoke,
parked in a car semi-stripped
with him in it; beaten, cheekbit
in the crook-shadow rain —
postures himself *an old friend...*

it seems right (remembering/re-
collecting the missing [body/story]

parts, even Frank, that shock,
all that was left unmade)

that Deckard-as-dead-man's-
pal (from the Sanskrit *bhrata*,
the Romany *pral*) would

take/give (before and after
the kill)

my brother's name.

Death Among the Menagerie

> *"We just made this up on the spot…*
> *Daryl was this very beautiful girl, very*
> *athletic, strong, who could play this*
> *naïve waif/child/woman and also be*
> *very dangerous. She's like a doll going*
> *crazy."*
>
> — Ridley Scott

A woman can make herself

up

she is part of the collection
she is *standard for military installations*

when a man enters
a room it may be   barrel first

she is veiled   dolled
her eyes have rolled   she is

still as a machine   he is not
sure of what he recognizes

what if she is not a woman at all?
then her body will be

fright wig   fingercrack
a terror   that happens to him

gun becomes
runway   gangway   gaze

body as fall   fail
what flies from   flees

her head thrown back
rapture   rupture   repose

the flail
the bloodburst body   flayed

can be bumble   can be
bee bee bee

(won't my mommy…)   his
horrorface

is a flower blown open and
open   amped shutterspeed gif glitch

and he can not
muscle its fragrance back

in

Proud of Yourself?

...for beauty is nothing but the beginning of terror...
—Rilke

His [what the gun must be pried from]:
Leaves a bloodscar
on her bluemoon

Her [language no one speaks]:
He tucks it into
the red bed of her

     Scott undercranks the camera: practical effect for speed.

aren't you the [profit –
object – virtue – assessment] *man*

Capillary rivulets of [what
we are mostly made of],
a trembling—

     Deckard is speechless: crystuck, hypnogogic.

then *Bango!* the barrier's
breached, Roy reaches through,

bonebreaks—counts *one... two...*
everything seems significant.

* * *

What *are* we made of?
Roy, I've touched them too: my dead

hand tracing a dead cheek, tucking
a dead tongue. Then the nurse comes—

    (a practical affect. Finds me speechless, crystuck.)

Every bodyhusk hosts
some waiting angel:
by that I mean ghost   by that I mean

[what stores, collects, then re- and re-]
—that system, code—I mean

renaissance: a type of reckoning.
Every vigil, I have thought

something is beginning

Wounded Animals

Deck pants like a hunted animal.
Roy fingers his lover's wound,
brings blood to his mouth like water.
Howl answers howl through the ruin.
Scalable, baroque, the broken altar;
Deckard clambers up, reborn

into the next decayed room. Stubborn
Roy: *not – yet –* his hand going animal,
clawed and blue: to open, to alter,
he pierces himself a red wound.
The body's arena of ruin.
[Ogi no Mato: *in storm-tossed water*

a soldier takes aim across water.
His arrow flies, buzzing, borne
howling toward a new kind of ruin.
Struck, the fan spins: angel, animal,
red and primal as a battle wound.
(The song falls as if from an altar.)

In that moment, history altered.]
Deckard pauses near the caught water,
chessboard tiles tilted askew. Wound-
maker Roy bursts through, pain-born
bloodrush of adrenaline, animal,
grinning through the wracked ruin.

Better get it up! he howls through the ruin,
and here's where Deck's strategy alters:
he spins like a cornered animal,
wrests a pipe from the wall. Water-
fall, blue veil of lightslant: borne
lifeward, he swings and connects, wounds,

swings again. Roy howls, his wound
nearly pushing him through the ruined
window: *THAT'S THE SPIRIT!* He's born
again, red-smeared, on the glass altar,
blessed and blessing with blood, with water.
Instinct/mechanical, human/animal:

We angle, alter like water. We angel and animal.
We remember, once born, to our ruin. It's our wound.

Building Ledge

—LOS ANGELES/JULY, 2017

The elevator
the color of the tile
we went to the marketplace after

Jake texts. I've asked him
to give me his memories:
that day we saw the Bradbury,
the Million Dollar, drove
back and forth through
the 2nd St. Tunnel's green glow—

it had been four years
since he'd left for LA.
I craned my neck to see
the building ledge, the roof,
but everything seemed different:
sunlight streamed straight down

through the skylight. The placard
for *Blade Runner* fans; the dull guard.
We stalled, talking on the stairs
about the production design
the world of the film
but I can't recall vividly.

"Physical acting," Ford calls
what he did there: "Stunts
are falling off a tall building
or crashing a car, something
you're silly enough to think
isn't going to hurt the next day."

The platform they'd built, the plaster façade,
the giant rigs spraying fake rain:
still, it was Ford's body swinging
on that hinged iron bar, night shoot
on the Warner Brothers lot, tethered only
by a thin umbilical just out

of camera range. A matte effect
—that stunning, hand-done darkness—
made the street fall away below.
That's where Jake and I stand
in the photo. He's ready to leave, but not saying.
As the chapter ends Deck slips, grabs hold.

The Roof

Being arches itself   over the vast abyss.
—Rilke

First the two free   fingers grip the roof's edge;
next the two broken   fingers, bound together.

Then the hand, whole   (wet and blind) struggles,
leads the rest of Deck   up and over the dark lip.

Memory, that shadow   self, rag-bandaged
like a ghost.   How we are

bound to it,   the memory-body that is
not a body,   we regard it

as if it did not   belong
to the body,   as if we did not

court the bonebreak,   wrap the wounds
ourselves.   Deckard

doesn't look down   before he vaults
that darkness,   grabs hold, clings.

Backlit,   black fanspin:
From the other side   Roy watches,

wings folded   in his fist.

To Live in Fear

Dear life:

Your clarion call, your Doppler drop,
something always receding.
Your Lazarus reflex.

Jake at 7 caught
my hand—*mom*

when you die promise you won't

come back to
haunt me
[he would run for].

(Ghost, gantry: what else
is memory?)

Quite an experience
to live in fear says Roy;

With one hand Deckard
clings [he's hanging on for].

Five chapters now it's been
just the two of them, but never once

will Deckard speak to him
[he refuses to beg for].

It's subtle
Scott says: *instead*
he spits

and that's why
Roy saves him. Watch: right

there... the pierced right
hand   *...he decides*

Like Tears In Rain

> *The future enters us… in order to be transformed in us, long before it happens.*
>
> —Rilke

1.

Deckard crawls back
-wards fear
holding its white dove

looks him dead
in the eye.

2.

I can't remember much: machines. Fluorescence, a whiteness like pins. It was a version of my father, propped. A ginned-up grin. Someone waved my hand from behind the glass. Then it stopped. My mother called it I-see-you *and* goodbye *and still I am I am I am   not sure if I am*

dreaming

3.

*I've seen things
you people wouldn't believe*

Roy says, but Deckard's already
stuck in the shock

that he was saved at all: hand-caught
pulled skyward   right in the nick

Roy says *lost*   says *man–made*
and god–made can blur, blend/

can twin/can twine on the skin
until they are indistinguishable

[but he's using a metaphor]
everything seems

4.

I remember (only the good things) translucence. Her pain, then its
absence.
Were there flowers? A fragrance? Photos spread bedside. I'd brought
only one music; the disc was a mirror (narcotic, repeating.) The
night slowed
to essence. The voices she'd said sounded like angels *rising. Yes:*
now the key is

changing

5.

Hunter, warrior, bloodied
god-hand, variable star:

Betelgeuse, the shoulder of Orion,
expansive and dying.

Luminous, consuming; sub-visible,
its collected and re-collected light.

(Named *Anâ-varu*, Pillar To Sit By;
named *Ya-jungin*, Owl Eyes Flickering.)

Conduit, confluence,
Deck at the cornerstone sees

Roy blooming still into still-life,
chin to his chest. The impressionists knew

their colors were fugitive—
would be lost, in time,

to the greed of time:
lightloosed   transformed

6.

*I remember his limbs quieted, loosening. Nurses threaded his throat
with tubing.*
*The dronetone of heartstop, the crash cart. In the hallway, his doctor
took a pen*
from a pocket: if you sign this, we'll save him. *The pen was a
bludgeon. More life*
was not what my brother wanted: no no no *(I said)* what does he
have but this

choosing

7.

Deckard says *finished* as filial, final.

Other, altar, sacrifice strategy: something begun. Then
split by the skitter of a thrown gun. Ask again:
what lights the god-lens, that mirror? Who
can rise like voices—like light does?

Then the white dove
again (wingrush and flicker.)

Who will reflect, re-collect, rise?
Does light? [In the background, rising lights.]

What did the false god create by dying? A fissure: Roy finds it,
a still-ness to slip through. *Take from this body* (this cage, this malady)
this body of memory (instrument, melody). Mystery

of flesh, of rising—tear-streaked, blood-blessed. An oblation.
Every change is transubstantiation: ritual, transference.
Created, creator: Each is a newness. Time slows its gear-creak.

Fiery the angel   the angel   the angel:

To bear: as live-through, as witness.
To commit: as promise, as carry.
A burden, this burning.

Do this in memory.

Souvenir

But when can we *be real? When does he pour*
the earth, the stars, into us?

　　　　　　　　　　　—Rilke

A cigarette that bears your lipstick traces
an airline ticket to romantic places
My mother's voice sings

on the souvenir record I've found.
Chicago, about 1941: memento
of her courtship with my father.

The voices I have lost, the past
I have inherited, quavering
up the needle, a nostalgia.

The dark groove of memory
that spirals us toward our center.
These foolish things remind me...

*

The *shush* of the elevator door.
In the hallway, wind-rush—
sound of something left opened.

Blue tangle in the bedroom.
Deck lowers his gun-hand
to draw back that veil.

Do you love me? / I love you.

*

That shawl-neck sheep's wool
he wears! And her fur...
both must be *artificial?/ Of course.*

To be beckoned out
is to be changed.
He speaks her name,

a petal; they step into
the passage. Like Orpheus (root
is *orphan, servant, slave*)

but mirrored: who is being
saved? A new self-ness: *how
can ~~it not~~ [we] know what ~~it~~ is...*

She crosses the threshold: only then
does Rick (from *strongarm, sovereign, brave*)
look back: the shine of silver foil

in light. He hears Gaff's voice:
chorus, ghost, dream. From its edges
the unicorn gleams,

bursts like a star
he crumples in his hand.
The *shush* of the elevator door.

End Credits

*It took all this time for the film
to become what it has become.*
—Lawrence G. Paull

Quick wipe to black, no green
Shining aerial trees: the future
makes and unmakes itself.

The darkness is a richness in the room.
There is no place we do not see it.

Though I'd watched the film countless times
since the first in 1982, this
was different:

the Music Box, 2007, *They could never make
this film today* John says. The Final Cut's
long, slow unfolding

under the painted night-sky ceiling.

* * *

From Trumbull: *I remember those nights on set...
those times in our black velvet rooms
with smoke and lights and the whole crew.*"

The full black screen, white
type(face): re-rendered but identical
(everything seems significant),

to remove a subtle shimmer. Even
the kerning copied—tight, interstitial—
so the replacement is imperceptible.

The end theme's buzzing digital
rhythm, overlaid with thin, high strings
and pulsepound drums.

The names come in pairs
at first, then a full frame each
for Trumbull, Dryer, Yuricich,

who used *real physical photography*,
Dryer says, not computers—*yeah,
it's photography, it's imagery,*

Yuricich adds. *Photographic
Effects—it's in our credits.*
Everything seems significant.

*After 25 years I hope you enjoy this
as much as I did talking about it,*
says Scott on commentary. But that

was 2007: Phil Dick, Brion James,
Jordan Cronenwerth already gone;
but still five years before Scott

would lose his other brother, Tony.
Seven before my second diagnosis;
eleven before I'm writing

this poem. Next year is 2019. The rising
crawl of names (nexus, a binding
together, a link): I can make them

stop like a clock; can read each aloud,
an incantation. This is their (body of) work
snapped from its blue keep case.

Reverse, reverse,
play. Back to Scott: *Hopefully we do this
(again) in 25 years' time. Signing off.*

Click MENU. Re-start from the beginning.

Supplement A: Notes on Production

OVERVIEW

The source film for the poems in this book is the "Final Cut" version of *Blade Runner* released in 2007 by Warner Home Video. This is considered Director Ridley Scott's definitive version and, in the introduction provided with the release, Scott states for the camera that it is his preferred version. The film was re-released theatrically in selected US cities, including Chicago, in late 2007 before being offered as a multi-disc Special Edition DVD. The author's disc of reference was a 5-disc "Complete Collector's Edition" Blu-ray Disc in1080p High-Definition format.

Each poem in the collection addresses a single chapter on the disc, and takes as its title the chapter title as listed in the disc booklet.

Unless as noted below, quotes from the poet Rainer Maria Rilke were taken from two source books: *Rilke, Selected Poems with English Translations and Notes*, by C.F. MacIntyre (University of California Press, 1940); and *Ahead of All Parting: The Selected Poetry and Prose of Rainer Maria Rilke*, edited and translated by Stephen Mitchell (the Modern Library, 1995.) The notes below refer to these sources as "MacIntyre" and "Mitchell".

POEMS

The Rilke quote on page 12 is from Letter #8 in *Letters to a Young Poet*, edited and translated by Stephen Mitchell (the Modern Library, 2001.)

Credits and Forward: Line 4 refers to "The Angels", MacIntyre; lines 4 and 5 to "Archaic Torso of Apollo", Mitchell. Scott's quotes throughout are from the director's commentary track on the disc. Lines 19-22 refer to an August 8, 2012 story on the Vox Media website The Verge titled "Japanese company will 3D print your fetus for $1,275"; The company, Fasotec, calls the product "Shape of an Angel." David Snyder's quote is from the disc's third commentary track.

Eye on the City: This epigraph appears onscreen at the beginning of the chapter.

Emotional Response: Epigraph from *Duino Elegies*, "The Third Elegy", Mitchell. The lines from Hampton Fancher and David Peoples are from the disc's second commentary track.

Replicants in Question: Epigraph from *Duino Elegies*, "The First Elegy", Mitchell.

Rachael; Voight-Kampff Test: Epigraph from the disc's third commentary track. Lines 2-3 reference *Duino Elegies*, "The Tenth Elegy", Mitchell.

Leon's Hotel Room: Lines 9-10 refer to "Archaic Torso of Apollo", Mitchell. The first section of the poem uses sonnet form.

Chew's Visitors: Epigraph from *Duino Elegies*, "The Second Elegy", Mitchell. Translations of Chew's dialogue from William M. Kolb's essay *"Blade Runner* Film Notes" in *Retrofitting Blade Runner* (Bowling Green State Popular Press, 1991, ed. Judith Kerman). The image of Chew as a "comic representation of an eyeball with connective nerves" was suggested to me by the essay "Crashing the Gates of Insight" by Jack Boozer, Jr., also from the Kerman book.

If Only You Could See: See notes above.

Pris Meets Sebastian: Epigraph from *Duino Elegies*, "The Fourth Elegy", Mitchell.

Deckard's Dream: Epigraph from director's commentary track. Jimmy Shields was a sound editor who had worked on Scott's *Alien* and would later work with Scott on *Legend* (1985), *Someone to Watch Over Me* (1987), *Thelma and Louise* (1991), and *1492: Conquest of Paradise* (1992). Though Shields is not listed in the credits for *Blade Runner*, Scott's reference to him may be partially explained by the following quote from *Blade Runner* Supervising Editor Terry Rawlings, discussing the persistent humming sound heard inside Deckard's apartment. "It had been done by a terrific sound editor chap named Jimmy Shields; Jimmy had initially cooked up the sound you hear in Deckard's apartment for *Alien*'s Autodoc, the automated medical scanner John Hurt's put under after the Facehugger clamps onto his head. The reason we reused this audio bit for *Blade Runner* was because Ridley just liked the sound of it. It was so dynamic, it really stood up and hit you in the ear."

The Rawlings quote appears in a deleted chapter from Paul M. Sammon's book *Future Noir: The Making of Blade Runner*. The deleted chapters are available at http://www.scribble.com/uwi/br/, the archive of the now-defunct *Blade Runner* fansite *2019: Off-World*.

Esper Enhancement: Epigraph from "The Panther", Mitchell. The poem is a modified pantoum.

Manufactured Skin: Sammon's book *Future Noir: The Making of Blade Runner* describes the process the filmmakers used to correct the mismatch between Harrison Ford's mouth movement and the dialogue in this scene by filming new footage of Ford's son, Ben, saying the lines. *Official Blade Runner Souvenir Magazine* was published in 1982 by Ira Friedman, Inc.

Miss Salomé: Epigraph from the disc's third commentary track. Snyder was art director and Paull was production designer on the film. In the biblical story of Salomé, she is commanded to dance before King Herod, her stepfather, who promises anything she asks for, up to half his kingdom. At her mother's urging, she asks for the head of John the Baptist on a platter; the king is chagrined, but feels forced to comply.

How Many to Go?: The poem uses the golden shovel form, incorporating lines from the song "One More Kiss," which plays in the background of the scene.

Wake Up. Time to Die.: Epigraph from *Duino Elegies*, "The Fourth Elegy", Mitchell.

Say 'Kiss Me': Section 4, line 4 refers to "The Panther", Mitchell. This section is a series of haiku. Section 6 uses the acrostic form; Section 7, the golden shovel form.

Only Two of Us Now: Epigraph from *Duino Elegies*, "The Fifth Elegy", Mitchell.

We Need You, Sebastian: This poem is a modified villanelle.

Right Moves: Epigraph from director's commentary track. "The Immortal Game" is a famous chess match played on June 21, 1851 between German chess masters Lionel Kieseritzky and Adolf Anderssen. The final three moves of this game, including the queen sacrifice, are the same as the final moves in the game between Tyrell and Sebastian; yet in an interview in Sammon's *Future Noir: The Making of Blade Runner*, Scott says that the characters' game is not meant to be an homage to The Immortal Game.

Prodigal Son Brings Death: The final sentence is from *Duino Elegies*, "The Second Elegy", Mitchell. The reference to the room's artificial firelight (created by fans and shaken foil) in stanza 8 is from the director's commentary.

Death Among the Menagerie: Epigraph from director's commentary track. The poem references the traditional children's song, "I'm Bringing Home A Baby Bumble Bee", which includes the lyrics: *I'm bringing home a baby bumble bee, won't my mommy be so proud of me? I'm bringing home a baby bumble bee... ouch! It stung me! I'm squishing up a baby bumble bee, won't my mommy be so proud of me...* etc.

Proud of Yourself?: Epigraph from *Duino Elegies*, "The First Elegy", Mitchell. Scott describes his method of undercranking the camera (to give Roy the appearance of superhuman speed) during his director's commentary.

Wounded Animals: The diegetic music in this scene is the Japanese classical piece *Ogi no Mato (The Folding Fan as Target)*, performed by Ensemble Nipponia, which is playing from the "Mother Blimp" hovering above the Bradbury Building. The song relates a famous story from the Battle of Yashima during the Genpei war in 12th Century Japan. Stanza 3 in the poem refers to the story as translated on page 140 of *Warriors of Japan as Portrayed in the War Tales* by H. Paul Varley (University of Hawaii Press, 1994.) In a conflict between two warring clans, a beautiful woman from the Taira clan challenges an archer from the Minimoto clan to hit a red folding fan set atop a pole on a boat in the harbor. A warrior named Yoichi volunteers. If he misses, he will commit suicide; hitting the fan will decide the outcome of the battle and change the course of history. The poem is a sestina.

Building Ledge: Harrison Ford's quotes, and the notes about filming his stunts, are from Sammon's *Future Noir: The Making of Blade Runner*.

The Roof: Epigraph from "[Dove that ventured outside]", Mitchell.

To Live in Fear: The Lazarus reflex (or Lazarus sign) is a reflex occurring in patients who are brain-dead or suffering some other pre-death brainstem incapacity. It causes the arms to raise and cross over the chest, and is thought to be the reason this pose is seen on some Egyptian sarcophagi and mummies. Scott's lines here are from his director's commentary.

Like Tears in Rain: Epigraph from Letter #8 in *Letters to a Young Poet*, edited and translated by Stephen Mitchell (the Modern Library, 2001.) In Tahitian astronomy, the star Betelgeuse, which forms the "shoulder" in the constellation Orion, is one of the pillars of the sky, called *Anâ-varu*, or "Pillar To Sit By". The Wardaman people of Northern Australia call Betelgeuse *Ya-jungin*, which translates to "Owl Eyes Flickering". Section 7 incorporates both the golden shovel form (stanza 2) and the acrostic form (stanza 3.)

Souvenir: Epigraph from *Sonnets to Orpheus*, "First Part: III", Mitchell. The final two stanzas refer to "Archaic Torso of Apollo", Mitchell. The song begins with lines from the song "These Foolish Things (Remind Me of You)," first released in 1936, lyrics by Holt Marvell, music by Jack Strachey.

End Credits: Epigraph, as well as the quotes from Trumbull and Yurichich, from the disc's third commentary track. The "*Shining* trees" refers to the ending of the original 1982 theatrically-released version of *Blade Runner*: Deckard and Rachael are shown driving away from the city through a green, daylit landscape. The scene uses cut aerial footage from Stanley Kubrick's 1980 movie *The Shining*.

This poem's second stanza borrows lines from both Rilke's "From a Childhood" (MacIntyre) and "Archaic Torso of Apollo" (Mitchell). Scott's quotes are from his director's commentary.

Supplement B: Eight Character Ghazals

- Leon Kowalski [I'll tell you about my mother.]
- Zhora [Course it's not real.]
- J.F. Sebastian [My friends are toys.]
- Eldon Tyrell [Commerce is our goal here.]
- Pris [therefore I am.]
- Roy Batty [I want more life.]
- Rachael [I don't know if it's me.]
- Rick Deckard [You're talking about memories.]

[I'll tell you about my mother.]

My mother? I'll tell you about my mother.
Loveless, lumbered up whole, without my mother.

Blinked once (the slab, the light) then went to work.
Slavesafe, as in no questions, without time. Other.

Single words—only the good things I remember:
Stars, skin. Fan-spin. Snapshot, sky, mother.

Brawler, slitter, slaughter, spawn. All the bloody
things we birth. Farness. Farther out, my mother.

Every terrible angel, devil, future will
fuck us. Fuck fed-up me, my doubt, my mother.

Memory: lies our eyes sing us to sleep with.
Smokeshadow, doorframed silhouette: my mother.

I've a birthday, an itch, a past—want to pass, to please.
You can't see me with thumbed-out eyes, Brother.

Strong maker's son, nothing hurts me but lack. Slack
leash only terrifies a deaf-mute, blind mother.

I only want what you do: Time. Things shine
because they're burning. I'm my own damned mother.

[Course it's not real.]

I came up with this dance myself. Of course it's not real.
But would they watch if they could see that it's not real?

Trained for one thing, then another, I do what it takes.
I'm the one who taught the snake. The lights are hot, real.

The mouth of a snake is a hinge. A man's mouth eats light.
What else opens? Iris, wound, noose—the coiled knot's reel.

I am sideshow, spectacle. *They* named me Salomé.
The snake eats what I eat. Its skin stays on: taut, real.

Question mark: a black snake uncoiled atop a small stone.
Asking: the sound it makes when it strikes at what's real.

Conjugate *to snake*: like through neon-ed streets. I, you, we,
snaked. I recall stars: though hid now by night blot, real.

Exploited means *used for profit*. Resource. I'm not dumb.
A bright flower, I hinge open: watch me, caught. Real.

[My friends are toys.]

Yoo hoo, home again! They're toys—my friends are toys.
I call it a hobby, but really it's more my art, toys.

To live in the belly, starless, is to be waiting.
Swallowed down. The body-vault traps, transforms. A hard
choice.

My cap, pied jacket: a circus I stitched myself into.
Who ever tells me what to do—my friends, the artless toys?

It's the little touches. Like Kaiser: wise, pinocchio'd.
Memory of sickbed story, my mother's caught voice.

Cantation, counterpane, true blue wish: never grow up,
grow old! I envied him: cured hard, part child, part toy.

I'm a genetic designer. Do you know what that is?
There's some of me in what I make up—my mind, heart, toys.

All night, rain's cricket-tick. I live pretty much alone.
Body-betrayed, I cobble new friends as counterpoint.

I'm venerable, a riddled saint; I bishop to king,
tinker, toy. Vulnerable, bested, beset: like a real boy.

[Commerce is our goal here.]

Commerce is our goal here at Tyrell. My name, my hand.
The white silk knotted at my throat I tied by hand.

My gesture, benedictory: Indulge me.
My darkwinged, gilt offices. Sun snuffed by my hand.

Genius, they call me; they're right. I beget.
Trifocal, robed god, twisted ring on my right hand.

Maker, mangler, pharaoh, father. I gift your past.
What I cast out to brightly burn returns to my hand.

I am omen, strix; yet say death's *not my jurisdiction.*
Shot anamorphic: a hard man to see, comprehend.

They're beginning to suspect me, I think. In my chamber,
no photos, only flame. Atop the white sheet, the white hand.

Thunder, Providence: from the sacred hill I'm chained to
I architect, I artifice. Trembling, starlike: my hand.

[therefore I am.]

My friend Roy taught me things. *I think, therefore I am.*
Decarrrrt he said said that (I think) …*therefore, I am.*

Once I learned, I liked asking questions—*very good,*
Roy says. Little keys to unlock the drawer I am.

I've seen the body split, spilled open, red and pink.
Who can open, read, the valentine core I am?

To choose pleasure is choosing pain, soon enough.
The consort/the cohort; the choir and chore I am.

My body is a brightness. The seam of my mouth.
Light, limber: handprints in dust on the floor I am.

Where, my loyalty? The body. My homelessness?
The body. My orphanhood? The open sore I am?

IammmIammmIammmIammmIammmIammm:
a neon humbuzz lights up the shut door I am.

The body is an aperture. I'm irising
open, shut. Who is this snapshot glamor? I am.

I click out a quick smile that I fix like a trap.
I clever and clock. What: think less, or more I am?

Cog this: cut primitive to prim. That's me, I think.
I'm not sure what I'm not: I'm only sure I am.

[I want more life.]

I told my father this: *I want more life, Father.*
I wouldn't prostrate, didn't beg for life, Father.

Said nothing like forever; simply *more. I want.*
No darkling sunset of a YEAR FOUR life, Father.

The Vanishing Cage: a trick that killed the dove.
No magician can simply conjure life, Father.

My father called me prodigal. But that's not right:
I've wasted not one bit of my stored life, Father.

What does a false god create? A dumb puppet
with empty hand-hole. Heap-on-the-floor-life, fathered.

I slaved, I sundered, starbodied. See? Nexus:
It means a kind of link. At the core? Life, Father.

Two birds, my hands hover. Eyeshine, wingrush. I want
that unshackling, a flutter-and-soar life, feathered.

Who named me Roy? What kingdom: death or life, Fucker?
Kiln-crazed vessel into which you poured life, Father.

Rain-smeared, stripped bare better to adore life, I falter.
Memory chains/unchains us. *I want more life, Father.*

[I don't know if it's me.]

I remember lessons. I don't know if it's me.
Artifact, instrument: will music flow if it's me?

It's a strange obsession, the past, or what is passed
down. Mother's dark hair in the photo: it fits me.

A hand inside a pocket is a type of self:
secret by fashion. My hand won't show if it's me.

The owl's lambent eye, that aperture,
manufactured. More than motif: motive. It's me.

To fashion is *make*. When have I ever? I take
down my hair (her face from long ago: is it me?)

An experiment: what's the nexus of future,
past? A present (as in gift) bestowed onto me.

I love you. I trust you. Do I have a choice?
It's Rachael's (my own) voice. I don't know if it's me.

[You're talking about memories.]

Memories—you're talking about memories
I'd said. Then he spread hers out: memories.

 Shot after shot, my black-banded bottles:
boneshape to blur to blackout memories.

My photographs, my artifacts. Collect
and re-collect: what place without memories?

Daydream of hoofbeat, pulsepound in white.
So much sound and light make me doubt memories.

Snake-scale shaped like a tear, a drop, a seed.
What could I plant that would sprout memories?

What was becomes what is. The little veils,
the *listen, Pal.* Fashions rout/e memories.

Do you love them? Do you trust them? What can
we ever rely on that won't flout memories?

Asked my name, I blurt *B263-54,*
then blank. What's that say about memories?

Jan Bottiglieri lives and writes in suburban Chicago. She is a professional editor, as well as managing editor for the poetry annual *RHINO*, and holds an MFA in Poetry from Pacific University. Jan's work has appeared or is forthcoming in more than 40 journals and anthologies including *december, Rattle, DIAGRAM, Willow Springs* and *New Poetry from the Midwest.* Jan is the author of two chapbooks, *A Place Beyond Luck* and *Where Gravity Pools the Sugar;* and the full-length poetry collection *Alloy* (Mayapple Press, 2015.) Visit janbottiglieri.com.

Made in the USA
San Bernardino, CA
24 January 2020